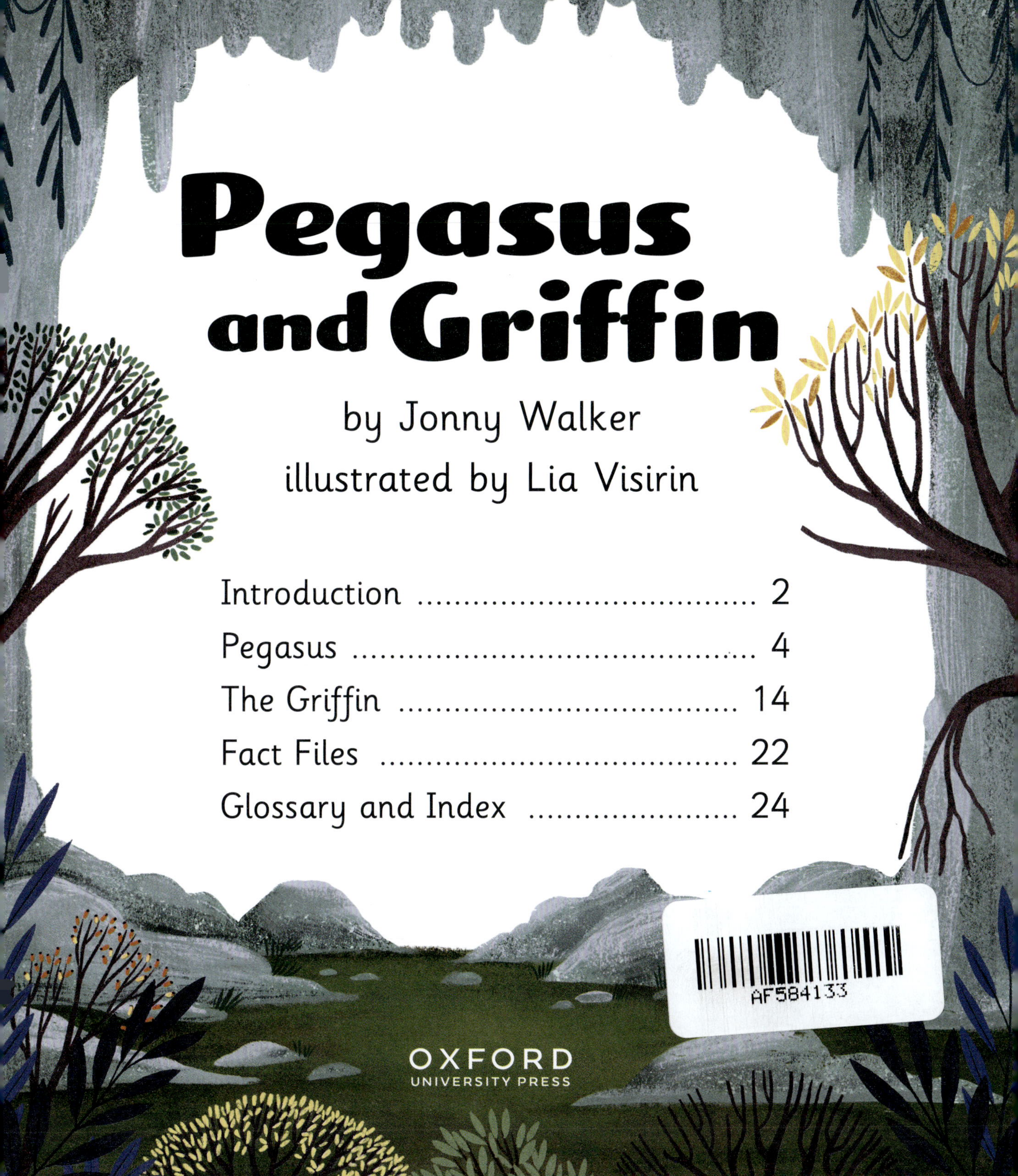

Pegasus and Griffin

by Jonny Walker

illustrated by Lia Visirin

OXFORD
UNIVERSITY PRESS

Introduction

In this guide, you will encounter a pair of fascinating creatures. Pegasus and the Griffin are beasts that exist in our imaginations. They are kept alive in old and fantastic tales.

Let's daydream about these beasts together. Let's pretend they exist for real. Which one would you like to meet?

Pegasus

The body of Pegasus

Pegasus is a peaceful and amazing beast. It looks like a powerful horse with the wings of a dove.

Most of Pegasus's body is ice-white. It looks as if it is wearing a blanket of snow. Its huge wings cast a shadow over its muscly body.

The wings of Pegasus

Pegasus's vast wings are made up of thousands of shimmering feathers. Many of these feathers are even longer than your outstretched arm.

A horse in flight is a spectacular sight. With great swoops of its wings, Pegasus can **ascend** into the skies. In a flash, Pegasus is gone!

Pegasus ascends. The beating of its wings creates great gusts of wind.

The special hooves of Pegasus

Pegasus's hooves have special powers. When they land on the ground, they create freshwater streams.

It is said that drinking from the streams can make you creative. People have sipped these special waters to fill their brains with ideas.

Where Pegasus lives

Pegasus hides between the ferns and tree trunks of the forest. No disguise is needed to help it hide. It moves quietly and quickly. It can never be spotted.

The shady forest lets it roam unseen.

People have guessed for a long time about where Pegasus came from. Did it **evolve** from horses? Or is it as old as time itself? No one knows for sure.

What Pegasus eats

Pegasus chomps the wild snacks it finds in the forest. It remains healthy by eating herbs and flowers.

It can always sniff out the **scent** of herbs and flowers.

The Griffin

The body of the Griffin

The Griffin is half-eagle and half-lion. It is a powerful and ferocious looking creature.

The Griffin has the strength and abilities of a lion and an eagle. It is known as the 'King of the Land and Sky'.

The wings of the Griffin

The wings of the Griffin are similar to a bird of **prey**. Its wings allow it to fly at dizzying speed.

Compare it with Pegasus's wings on page 6. How are they alike?

As it darts past the clouds, the Griffin lets out ghastly screams. The deafening sound acts as a caution. This creature fears nothing – and it is coming!

Where the Griffin roams

The Griffin keeps busy by constantly searching for gold. It roams in caves and mines, clawing and digging into the rocks. It can react angrily if it's disturbed when mining for gold.

When it has collected its gold, the Griffin hides it. Sometimes it is hidden beneath boulders. The Griffin guards it from above. It sits on the top of mountains, watching over its gold.

What the Griffin eats

The Griffin is a highly-skilled **predator**. It eats whatever animals it can find. It sprints after hares and foxes on the land.

It enjoys the challenge of a difficult chase. The Griffin will even hunt when in flight.

Fact File

Pegasus

Scores out of 100

Wing Size	95
Muscles	80
Secret Powers	95
Speed	60
Hunting Ability	5

Fact File
The Griffin
Scores out of 100
Wing Size 85
Muscles 60
Secret Powers 25
Speed 80
Hunting Ability 70

Glossary

ascend: to climb or fly up
evolve: to change slowly over a long time
muscles: parts inside the body that become tight or loose, to help the body move
muzzle: the nose and mouth part of a horse
predator: an animal that hunts other animals
prey: an animal that is hunted by another animal for food
scent: the way that something smells
torso: the main part of the body between the neck and hips

Index